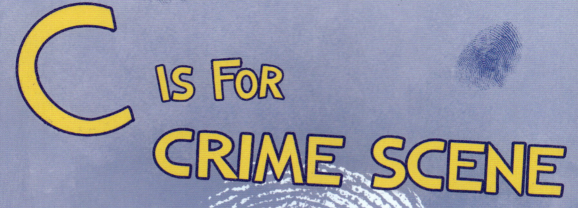

C is for Crime Scene

A Forensics A to Z Book

Written by **Dr. Judy Staveley**

Illustrated by **Alessandra Vitelli**

Science, Naturally!
An imprint of Platypus Media, LLC

Washington, D.C.

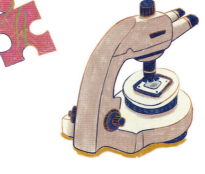
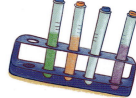

C Is for Crime Scene: A Forensics A to Z Book
Hardcover first edition • September 2025 • ISBN: 978-1-958629-91-8
eBook first edition • September 2025 • ISBN: 978-1-958629-92-5
Paperback edition coming soon.

Written by Judy Staveley, Text © 2025
Illustrated by Alessandra Vitelli, Illustrations © 2025

Project Manager, Cover and Book Design: Hannah Thelen, Washington, D.C.
Editors: Violet Antonick, Washington, D.C.
           Skyler Kaczmarczyk, Washington, D.C.
           Caitlin Burnham, Washington, D.C.

Editorial Assistants:
    April Garnock
    Daryn Schvimmer
    Gweneth Kozlowski
    Sudeeksha Dasari

Teacher's Guide available at the Educational Resources page of ScienceNaturally.com.

Published by:
    Science, Naturally! - An imprint of Platypus Media, LLC
    1140 3rd Street NE
    Suite 2005
    Washington, DC 20002
    202-465-4798
    Info@ScienceNaturally.com • ScienceNaturally.com

Distributed to the book trade by:
    Baker & Taylor Publisher Services (North America)
    Toll-free: (888) 814 0208
    Orders@BTPubServices.com • BTPubServices.com

Library of Congress Control Number: 2025931300

10 9 8 7 6 5 4 3 2 1

Schools, libraries, government and non-profit organizations can receive a bulk discount.
Contact us at Info@ScienceNaturally.com for more information.

The front cover may be reproduced freely, without modification, for review or non-commercial educational purposes.

All rights reserved. No part of this book may be reproduced in any form without the express written permission of the publisher.
Front cover exempted (see above).

Printed in China.

"For all the future forensic scientists, may your passion for truth and justice lead you to uncover the stories that evidence tells."
—**Dr. Judy Staveley**

"I dedicate this book to all curious children, like my beloved Nick and Sam."
—**Alessandra Vitelli**

Meet a forensic scientist!

When a crime happens, how do you find out who did it?

Forensic scientists start by looking for clues. They put the clues together to see the whole picture, like solving a puzzle.

Let's see how you would solve a crime... from **A** to **Z**!

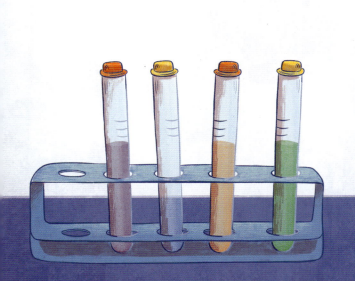

A is for Analyze

To solve a crime, you'll have to look around carefully to find clues.

B is for Blood

Look, there's a clue! Things left behind after a crime, like blood, can be used to find out who was there.

C is for Crime Scene

This is where the crime happened. Here, you'll collect clues that might help you piece together the mystery.

D is for DNA

Every person has a special code in their body called DNA. You can find DNA in blood or other clues, and it can be used to match a person to a clue.

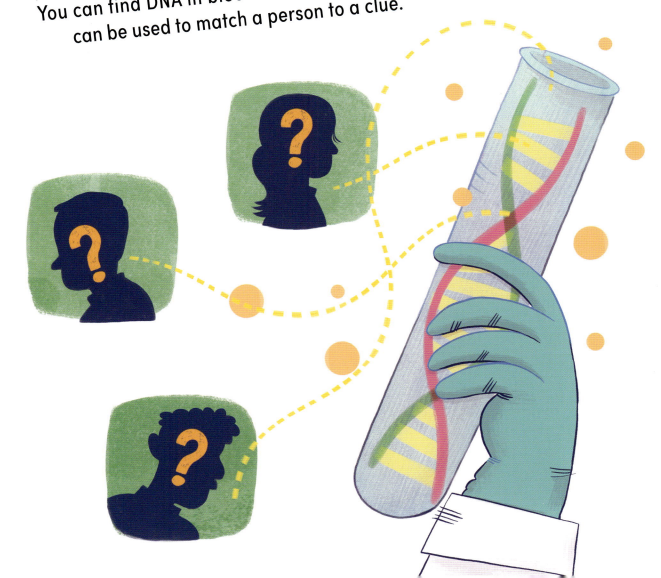

E is for Evidence

Evidence is what you call the clues that can help prove what really happened.

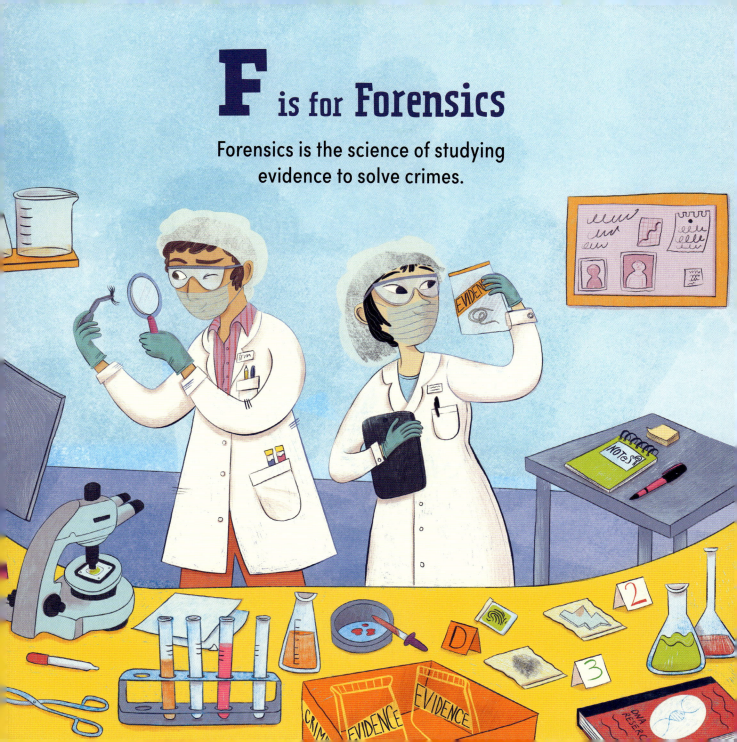

G is for Gloves

Wearing gloves keeps you safe and protects the clues, which could be important evidence.

H is for Hair

If you find hair at the crime scene, the details of how the hair looks can tell you about who it might belong to. You can also get DNA from a hair.

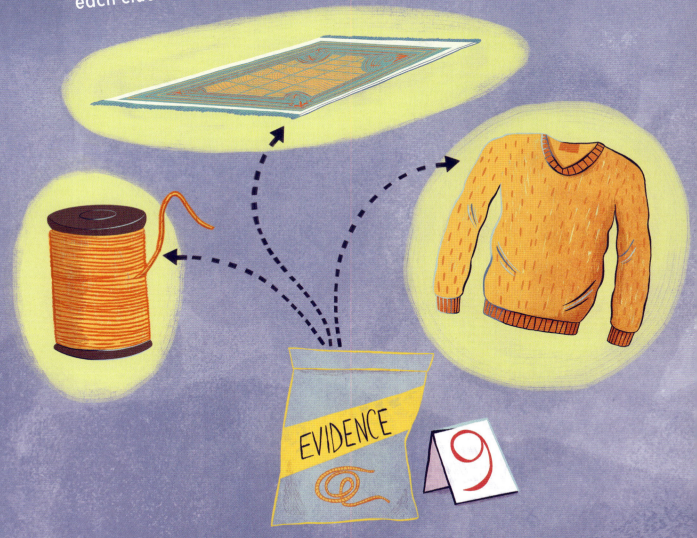

J is for Journal

In your journal, keep detailed drawings and notes. It will help you remember all the clues and what you know about them.

K is for Kit

As a forensic scientist, you will use the tools in your kit to gather clues.

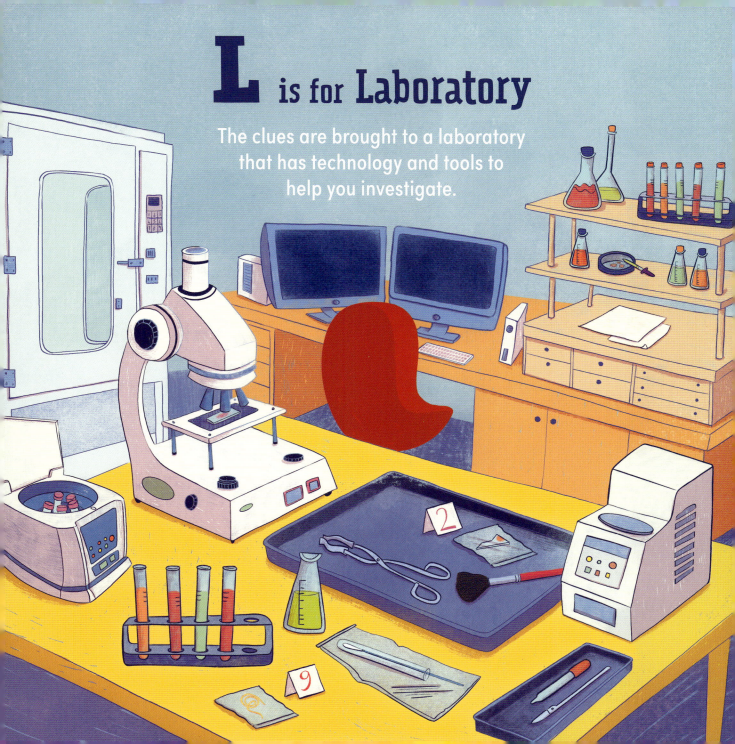

M is for Magnify

Some tools, like a magnifying glass or a microscope, let you look closer at a clue to see important details.

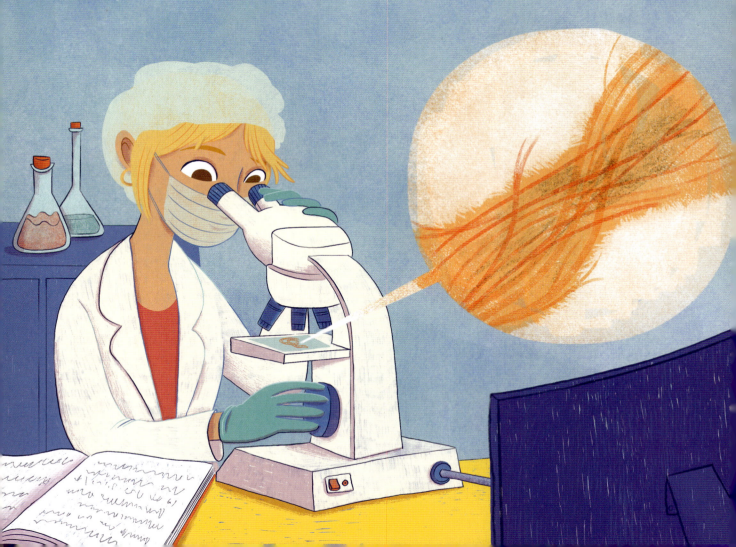

N is for New Lead

If you have a new idea about where a mysterious clue came from, then there's a new lead to investigate!

O is for Observe

Look over everything for details you might have missed. The smallest of clues could be the evidence that solves the mystery!

P is for Prints

Even fingerprints can be important evidence. They have unique patterns and DNA that can tell you who left them.

Q is for Questions

The best way to gather more evidence is to ask a lot of questions.

R is for Report

At the end of the investigation, forensic scientists write reports about what happened. But first, find as much evidence as possible!

S is for Swab

Using a swab from your kit, you can collect samples of clues like mud from the crime scene.

T is for Tracks

Tracks left behind are clues, too. These can be footprints that create a map of where people went during the crime.

U is for UV Light

Forensic scientists use these special lights to make hidden clues appear.

V is for Victim

A victim is a person who was hurt by the crime. To help them, forensic scientists do their best to find evidence and solve the mystery.

W is for Weapon

This is something that was used during the crime to cause damage. It's also important evidence.

X is for X-Ray

An x-ray machine lets you see inside the human body. Forensic scientists can use it to connect an injury to a weapon.

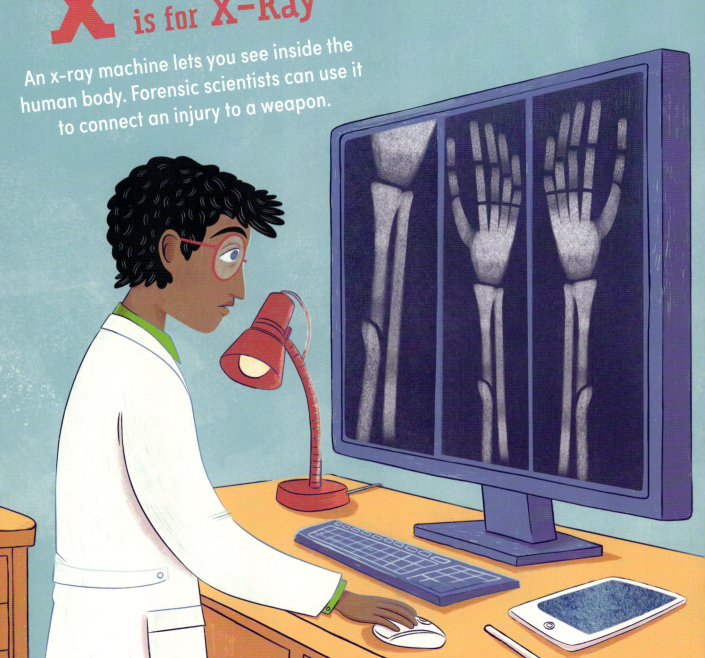

Z is for Zero Contamination

Yellow tape, gloves, and other special gear protect clues from being touched or damaged. That would be called contamination. Forensic scientists make sure there is no contamination, so all the evidence can be used to solve the crime.

CASE CLOSED

Could YOU solve a crime like a forensic scientist?

CASE Nº 1

AUTHOR

ILLUSTRATOR

Suspect no. 1
AUTHOR

Dr. Judy Staveley is a biotechnology expert and STEM consultant with advanced degrees in forensic science, biology, and health psychology. She has worked on biodefense and public health with federal agencies and has taught at multiple universities. Dedicated to mentoring future scientists, Dr. Staveley has directed the American Junior Academy of the National Association of Academies of Science and has served as President of the Washington Academy of Sciences. She loves being an athlete, learning, doing arts and crafts, and promoting STEM education. She lives in the Washington, D.C. area and can be reached at Judy.Staveley@ScienceNaturally.com.

Suspect no. 2
ILLUSTRATOR

Alessandra Vitelli is an Italy-based illustrator whose work focuses on the children's market. She has illustrated picture books, covers, education books, and magazines. Alessandra has also worked as a teacher at the Italian School of Comix in Naples since 2013. In addition to illustration, she is passionate about photography and typography. She currently lives in Naples, Italy, with her partner, two children, and two cats. She loves her large, cheerful, and sometimes noisy family. When not working, Alessandra enjoys traveling, reading, movies, and TV series (especially crime!).